POCKET BUILDER
PETS

Let's get building!

WRITTEN BY
TORI KOSARA

INTRODUCTION

This book is packed with ideas and tricks to help you become a better LEGO® builder—whether you're building for the first or the thousandth time. Start with the handy building tips on page 4. Then get out your LEGO collection, choose a page, and build! With advice and building techniques for making cute companions, pet homes, and animal accessories, you'll be a LEGO building expert in no time.

What sparks your imagination?

Chapter 2: Fantasy Friends

Chapter 3: Creature Comforts

Find me on page 58.

I carrot tell you how much fun this is!

BUILDING TIPS

Are you ready to start thinking like a LEGO® builder? Try some of these ideas, or come up with your own way of doing things. The most important thing to remember is to have fun!

This will be a mice thing to do!

GETTING STARTED

There's one thing you'll definitely need before you can build: LEGO pieces! Don't worry about the size of your collection or how new it is. The original LEGO® System in Play elements (made from 1958) fit perfectly with those made today. You can also buy second-hand LEGO pieces, share with friends and neighbors, or play with them at schools and libraries.

What size are these overalls?

SCALE UP OR DOWN

Decide what scale you want your model to be before you start so that you have the right number of LEGO pieces ready.

I'll sort this out.

SORT YOUR BRICKS

Organize your collection into element types and colors to save time as you build.

FIND A BUILDING SPACE

Look for a flat surface with plenty of room for building and storing your pieces, such as a table.

SWAP IT OUT

If you don't have the perfect piece, think about other parts you can use instead.

BUILD TOGETHER

Ask a family member or a friend to join in and share the joy of building. You might learn new things from each other!

Maybe I'll swap green for blue bricks!

CHOOSE YOUR COLORS

Use whatever colors you like when you're building. Your models can look however you want!

DON'T PANIC!

There is no right or wrong way to build. If your model doesn't turn out how you wanted it to, rebuild it or try something new.

KEEP BUILDING

The fun is in the building, so just keep connecting your bricks until things click for you.

Find me on page 12!

CHAPTER 1
PERFECT PETS

Let's hop to it and build!

COLORFUL CAT

Cats come in many shapes, sizes, and colors. This fuzzy feline has a patterned coat made from pieces in white, black, tan, and brown. But you could create a cat with fluffy fur in all the colors of the rainbow!

How will I get down from here?

Brown 1×1 slopes make convincing cat ears

Two minifigure claw pieces form the whiskers

BUILD TIP!

Build the body in sections—head, torso, and bottom. Then connect the sections.

Long, winding tail is an elephant trunk piece

FEET FIRST

Four flat feet made from rounded plates with bars make a sturdy base for this cat model. It can sit without toppling over.

1×1 plate

1×1 rounded plate with bar

HOWLING HOUND

What's your favorite kind of dog? There are lots of breeds (types) to choose from, such as this basset hound. Basset hounds have short legs and stout bodies. Will your dog have pointy ears or a stubby tail? Think about the features.

Has anyone seen my new bouncy ball?

2×3 wedge plates make long, floppy ears

1×4 arch forms both of the short front legs

1×1 half circle tiles are the right shape for dog paws

WAG ON

This happy hound has a waggly tail! A 1×2 brick with one side stud keeps the dog's tail centered in its body.

1×2 brick with one side stud

Dinosaur tail tip

JUMPY FROG

It's fun to watch pet frogs hop about and catch bugs with their long tongues. Be sure to build in plenty of playful features when you make a frog model like this one. Jump to it!

BUILD TIP!

Use a jumper plate to make the mouth. This way you can center the long tongue.

1×2 tile creates smooth, frog-like skin

Tile looks like a long, flicking tongue

Blue and green slope bricks shape the frog's squat body

1×1 round transparent tile with bar

Minifigure roller skate

1×2 plate

LICKETY STICK

The studs on the 1×2 plate at the end of the frog's tongue are perfect for holding snacks!

PERKY PARROT

Build yourself a chirpy companion, such as a parrot. You could even make a whole flock of feathered friends in different sizes and colors to keep you company. Get ready to spread your wings and put your LEGO® building skills to the test.

When it comes to building, just wing it!

Printed eye tiles fit onto 1×1 bricks with side studs

Two 2×3 wedge plates make sturdy feet

Pointy slope pieces make good birds' tails

BEAK UP

Wedges and slopes are good shapes for beaks. This slope attaches to two bricks with side studs.

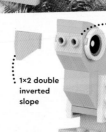

1×1 brick with side studs

1×2 double inverted slope

PETITE PIGLET

Pigs make popular pets because they can be easily trained. You can teach a pocket-size hog made from your LEGO collection plenty of tricks. This one already knows how to sit!

Ears can move up and down on clip and bar connections

Two wedge plates make cute little ears

What trick should I do next?

Round and rounded plates for a curly tail

CLEVER CONNECTION

There are two bricks with studs on all sides at the base of the model. Pieces can be added all around them.

1×2×1⅓ brick with side studs ·····

2×2 plate ·····

SQUIRMY SCORPION

Real scorpions don't like to be touched, but this LEGO version is happy to be played with or put on display. Make sure it has eight legs; two claws for catching brick-built prey (animals eaten as food); and a big, bendy tail.

Robot arm connects the scorpion's long, curved tail to its body

BUILD TIP!

Clip the tail and legs to the bars last to stop them falling off while you're building.

Plates and tiles form layers of armor-like protection

ARMED AND READY

The scorpion's spindly legs are actually made from skeleton arm pieces. They clip onto a round plate with bars.

2×2 round plate with octagonal bars ······

Skeleton arm ·····

CALM KOI

Many people keep koi (the Japanese word for carp) in peaceful ponds. These beautiful fish have long life spans of around 40 years. Your koi model could brighten up a brick-built pond for even longer than that!

Use slopes to create the fins for your model

I love my peaceful pond!

Minifigure boomerang makes barbels (whiskers)

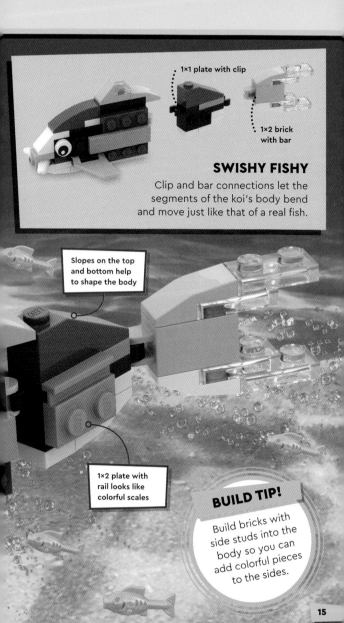

1×1 plate with clip

1×2 brick with bar

SWISHY FISHY

Clip and bar connections let the segments of the koi's body bend and move just like that of a real fish.

Slopes on the top and bottom help to shape the body

1×2 plate with rail looks like colorful scales

BUILD TIP!

Build bricks with side studs into the body so you can add colorful pieces to the sides.

TERRIFIC TOAD

Now you see her—now you don't! Many pet toads use their strong back legs to burrow into soil. Be sure to build sturdy limbs for your model so your pet can pretend to dig.

BUILD TIP!

Start with a baseplate for the belly and then build the toad upward in layers.

I make a toad-ally great pet!

Pins connect the printed eye tiles to the head

Studs create bumpy warts on the skin

1×1 round plates with leaves for webbed feet

···· Curved slope

···· 1×2 hinge plates

·········· 2×6 plate

JOINED AT THE HIP

Pairs of hinge plates at the toad's hips let the legs attach at angles. This creates a realistic look.

BRIGHT TROPICAL FISH

Add a burst of color to your home with a shoal of bright tropical fish like this one. There's no need to fuss with special equipment for these brick-built pals. Just build as many finned friends as you like and put them on display for all to admire.

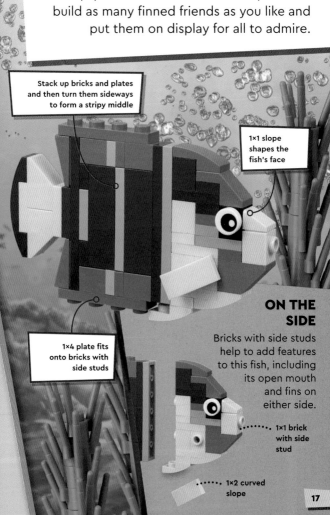

Stack up bricks and plates and then turn them sideways to form a stripy middle

1×1 slope shapes the fish's face

1×4 plate fits onto bricks with side studs

ON THE SIDE

Bricks with side studs help to add features to this fish, including its open mouth and fins on either side.

••••••• 1×1 brick with side stud

•••••• 1×2 curved slope

TINY TURTLE

You won't have to shell out all of your allowance to care for this petite pet. Once built, your turtle model doesn't need much—just space and time to play with you and your friends!

Smooth slope pieces make a realistic-looking turtle shell

What shell we do today?

1×2 inverted curved slopes for flipper-like feet

The turtle's head attaches to a 2×2 inverted slope

HALF SHELL
Build the base of the model in an oval shape. Then build upward to complete the shell.

1×2 brick

2×2 corner brick

SPINDLY SPIDER

If you've always wanted a fang-tastic spider as a pet, you can build one using your LEGO bricks! The spider can be as big or as small as you like. Just make sure it has eight legs, eyes, a rounded body, and two fierce fangs, of course!

BUILD TIP!

Make sure the spider's eight legs are equal in length. This will help it stand up.

Two curved slopes create a rounded shape

Thin legs can move up and down on clips and bars

2×2 slide plate

ITSY-BITSY SLIDER

2×2 slide plates keep the underside of the spider's body extra secure.

MARVELOUS MOUSE

This little mouse takes only a little time to make. Before you get started, find straight and curved slopes to help form the face and rounded rodent body. You'll have a sweet new pet in no time!

2×2 radar dishes for big, round mouse ears

Has anyone seen a piece of cheese?

Long, smooth dinosaur tail pieces

BUILD TIP!

Begin by building a base at the belly. Then build above and below to finish the model.

Plates with clips form four small, clawed feet

CUTE CURVES

Six curved slopes on the top and sides of the build give the mouse's body a rounded shape.

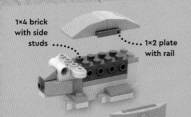

1×4 brick with side studs

1×2 plate with rail

2×2 curved slope

BOUNCY BUNNY

Spring into action and build a rabbit that's easy to care for. Much of the body—including the arms, legs, and even the snout—are made from small slopes. Remember to give your bunny two long, pointed ears, too.

Building makes me hoppy!

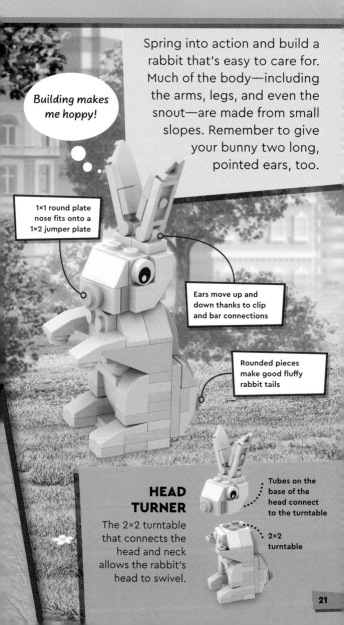

1×1 round plate nose fits onto a 1×2 jumper plate

Ears move up and down thanks to clip and bar connections

Rounded pieces make good fluffy rabbit tails

HEAD TURNER

The 2×2 turntable that connects the head and neck allows the rabbit's head to swivel.

Tubes on the base of the head connect to the turntable

2×2 turntable

SHAGGY SHEEP

"Wool" you build a barnyard buddy? Form a solid middle for the sheep by sandwiching bricks with side studs between plates. Then add the rest of the features, including a head, legs, tail, and a woolly coat.

This is un-baa-lievably fun!

Eyes are two 1×1 round printed tiles

Two slope pieces add a curved shape to the back

Stacks of 1×2 log bricks form the sheep's legs

2×2 wedge plate

2×3 plate

2×2 round plate with axle hole

1×2 plate with three claws

FLEECY FLOURISHES
Layers of white pieces in different shapes come together to form a fluffy-looking wool coat for the sheep.

ROWDY ROOSTER

Cock-a-doodle-*do* you want to make a model that's worth crowing about? Then grab your bricks and build a feathered farmyard friend to keep you company. Lots of curved pieces make the bird instantly recognizable.

1×2 curved slopes make the comb and wattle

2×2 curved slopes create a strong, puffy chest

BUILD TIP!

To add movement to the wings and tail, use clip and bar connections in your model.

1×2 wedge slopes form convincing rooster feet

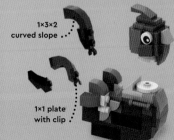

1×3×2 curved slope

1×1 plate with clip

TAIL FEATHERS

Curved slopes clip onto bars built into the bird's rear. Together, they form an impressive tail.

HOMEY HERMIT CRAB

To care for hermit crabs, you need to make sure they have protective shells to call home. So build a shell big enough for your brick-built pet crab's body to fit securely inside.

3×3×2 quarter dome pieces form the shell

BUILD TIP!

Build the shell first. Once the shell is finished, add the legs, eyes, and antennae.

Plates and curved slopes form crab-like legs

Two plates with clips look like crab claws

RING UP

Two horn pieces fit into a 1×1 plate with ring that attaches to the shell. This forms the crab's antennae.

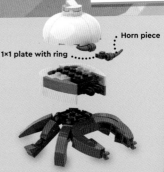

Horn piece

1×1 plate with ring

JUMPING GRASSHOPPER

Grasshoppers are incredible to watch! Their strong legs help them leap impressively long distances for an insect. If you decide to build a pet LEGO grasshopper like this one, be sure to give it sturdy legs to stand on. What are you waiting for? Leap to it!

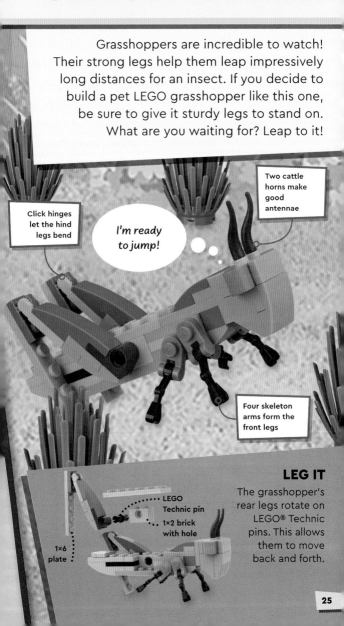

Click hinges let the hind legs bend

Two cattle horns make good antennae

I'm ready to jump!

Four skeleton arms form the front legs

LEGO Technic pin

1×2 brick with hole

1×6 plate

LEG IT

The grasshopper's rear legs rotate on LEGO® Technic pins. This allows them to move back and forth.

PATTERNED PEACOCK

Pet peafowl need large outdoor landscapes to roam about. But you won't need much room to keep a brick-built peacock at home. Gather your jewel-colored pieces and create an eye-catching companion.

Tall head plume is a 1×1 round plate with bar

BUILD TIP!

Plan out your feather pattern and set aside the pieces you need before you build.

1×2 rounded plate

3×4 plant leaf fits onto 4×8 half round plate

HANG AROUND

Two 1×2 rounded plates connect this impressive train to 1×1 round tiles with bars in the bird's body.

1×1 heart tiles decorate the peacock's large train (tail)

I'm a big fan of these birds!

Gold 1×1 round plates with leaves make pointy, feathered tips

DARLING DUCK

"Waddle" you play with an adorable duck like this one? Real pet ducks need plenty of space to swim about, but your brick-built bird is happy to hang out with you on dry land. Grab your bricks and get quacking!

Two 1×1 slopes form the tail feathers

1×2 jumper plate keeps the head centered

1×1 plate with tooth creates a wing tip

ABOUT FACE

A central 1×1 brick with side studs holds the duck's facial features and connects the bird's head to its body.

1×1 slope

1×1 brick with side studs

Printed eye tile

2×2 jumper plate

BUILD TIP!

A flat base will allow you to push your model along as though it's swimming.

NIFTY NEWT

Newts feast on creepy crawlies, such as worms. Thankfully, a LEGO newt doesn't need to eat anything. If you feel squeamish around squiggly, slimy things but you love newts, then you can build one instead!

Smooth, pointed tail is made from a barb piece

This building thing is newt to me!

1×1 round plates with holes for the sturdy rear feet

1×2 triple slope forms a pointy newt nose

1×1 plate with clip

1×1 rounded plate with bar

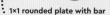

NODDING NECK

The newt's neck is a 1×1 plate attached to a piece with bar. This lets the head move up and down.

CHAPTER 2
FANTASY FRIENDS

There are no baa-aad builds!

HAPPY HOT DOG

Snap your bricks together to build a wiggly wiener dog complete with a cozy bun. Can you dream up other food-themed pets, such as a hamburger hedgehog or a cupcake kitten?

Round bricks form the hot dog's long body

Hot dog— I look good!

1×6 tile covers the studs on the 2×6 plate below

PLATE UP

The bun's curved slope sides attach to a 2×6 plate. This fits onto a brick with side studs in the hot dog's body.

1×2 brick with side studs

2×6 plate

2×2 curved slope

FLASHY LIGHTNING BIRD

Zap! This super-powered songbird soars on lightning bolt wings and sends electric shocks shooting from its beak and limbs. You could also pretend the transparent pieces are magical ice powers. Get creative and invent a super pet!

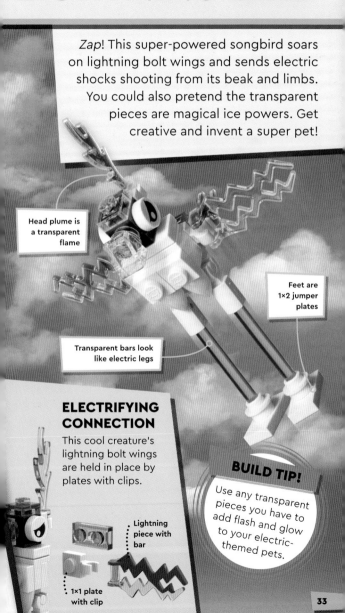

Head plume is a transparent flame

Feet are 1×2 jumper plates

Transparent bars look like electric legs

ELECTRIFYING CONNECTION

This cool creature's lightning bolt wings are held in place by plates with clips.

Lightning piece with bar

1×1 plate with clip

BUILD TIP!

Use any transparent pieces you have to add flash and glow to your electric-themed pets.

LOVELY LLAMACORN

Do you like llamas and unicorns? Combine them and invent your own magical creature, such as this llamacorn. It has a long neck like a llama and a unicorn's horn, of course!

BUILD TIP!

Find special pieces, such as a horn, to add a touch of magic to your models.

Horn fits securely in a 1×1 round plate with hole

Large printed eye tile attaches to a brick with side studs

Stack up standard bricks to make a stretchy neck

2×2 curved slope

1×2 plate

WIDE SIDE

One 2×2 curved slope attaches to the studs of a 1×2 plate built into the body. The slope adds width to the llamacorn.

Llamacorn hooves are made of plates with slopes

FANTASTIC BIRD-ZARD

Even fantasy creatures like this one—which is half reptile and half bird—need proper care. Be sure to take your brick-built pet pals to the LEGO® vet for a checkup. And remember to bring their favorite treats!

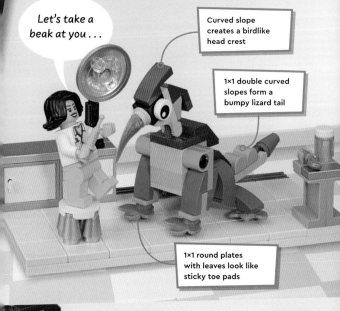

Let's take a beak at you...

Curved slope creates a birdlike head crest

1×1 double curved slopes form a bumpy lizard tail

1×1 round plates with leaves look like sticky toe pads

1×2 curved slope

LEGO® Technic pin

1×2 plate with pin hole

1×2 inverted curved slope

LEG UP

Curved pieces give the legs a rounded shape. The legs fit onto pins that let them move back and forth.

MAGNIFICENT MICRO PETS

No room at home for a pet? You can build a miniature creature with just a handful of pieces! The little penguin is made from just seven small elements. How many tiny pets will you make for your mini menagerie?

1×1 plate with clip looks like small bear ears

I hope lunch isn't small!

1×2×1⅓ curved arch shapes the bunny's back

1×1 round plate with petals for a frilly mane

BUILD TIP!

Small pieces, such as 1×1 slopes, bricks, and plates are just right for micro builds.

It's great fun to build tiny pets!

1×1 printed tiles or round plates make good eyes

1×1 plate with tooth for the penguin's feet

1×1 brick with side studs

1×2 plate

MINI MIDDLE

All but one piece of the micro penguin fit onto a 1×1 brick with side studs at the center of the model.

37

SUPER STEGOSAURUS

If you've ever dreamed of having a dinosaur for a pet, then get out your LEGO collection and make your dreams come true! You could build a spiky stegosaurus like this one, a terrific T. rex, or any dino you fancy!

Thagomizer (four tail spikes) is made of horn pieces

I could do with a spot of lunch.

Legs move back and forth on clips and bars

Toes are 1×1 slopes attached to plates

SPOT ON

The stegosaurus's spots and spikes attach sideways to the model's body. Pieces with side studs hold the spikes and spots in place.

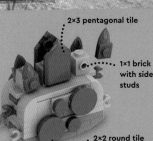

2×3 pentagonal tile

1×1 brick with side studs

2×2 round tile

RADIANT RAINBOWSAURUS

Scientists think that some dinosaurs may have been brightly colored. Piece together lots of bright patterns and invent your own pet dino with a body built in all the colors of the rainbow.

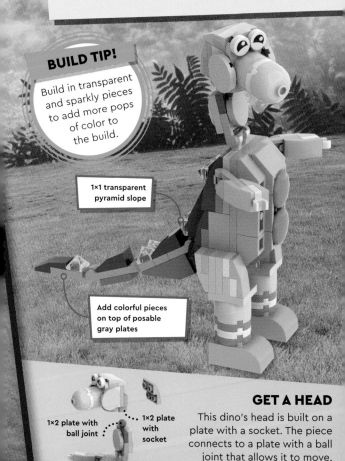

BUILD TIP!

Build in transparent and sparkly pieces to add more pops of color to the build.

1×1 transparent pyramid slope

Add colorful pieces on top of posable gray plates

1×2 plate with ball joint

1×2 plate with socket

GET A HEAD

This dino's head is built on a plate with a socket. The piece connects to a plate with a ball joint that allows it to move.

PADDLING PLESIOSAURUS

Bring the past to life with a prehistoric pet like this plesiosaurus, a water-dwelling reptile that lived at the time of the dinosaurs. Its long, posable neck is built in sections using clip and bar connections.

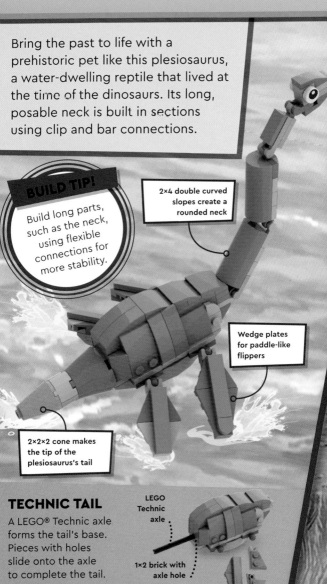

BUILD TIP!

Build long parts, such as the neck, using flexible connections for more stability.

2×4 double curved slopes create a rounded neck

Wedge plates for paddle-like flippers

2×2×2 cone makes the tip of the plesiosaurus's tail

TECHNIC TAIL

A LEGO® Technic axle forms the tail's base. Pieces with holes slide onto the axle to complete the tail.

LEGO Technic axle

1×2 brick with axle hole

POUNCING SMILODON

Smilodons may not have made the best house pets because they were powerful predators. But a saber-toothed LEGO smilodon can be a calm companion. Make sure to give yours long, sharp teeth and sturdy legs for running and pouncing.

4×4 wedge with a polygon top looks like shaggy fur

I'm looking pretty sharp!

2×2 curved slope shapes the top of the big cat's head

Long teeth are held in place by plates with clips

1×2 plates with teeth make fierce claws

STRONG LEGS

Slope pieces at the top and bottom of each leg add a muscular shape to the cat's powerful limbs.

1×3 inverted slope

1×2 slope

UNIQUE UNICORN

Build your own fictional friend based on a myth, legend, or fairy tale. There are no rules when it comes to creating imaginary pets. Go wild and make a one-of-a-kind brick-built fantasy creature like this unicorn.

What a legendary creation!

Two 1×1 slopes create a magical mane

Overlapping plates form a bright rainbow

Ball and socket connections make posable arms

1×1 double curved slopes for three of the unicorn's hooves

MYTHICAL TAIL

This unicorn's tail is made from a blue seaweed piece. It connects to a plate with bar, which fits into a clip at the rear.

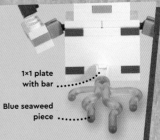

1×1 plate with bar ....

Blue seaweed piece ....

SLIPPERY SEA SERPENT

Ahoy, there! If you're looking for a pet to sail off on adventures with, then build a slithering sea serpent. You can make your sea serpent's posable body as long as you like.

Head spikes fit into the studs of jumper plates

BUILD TIP!

Build each section of the sea serpent's body separately. Then connect them.

Swirly vine piece could be a magical fin

Two wedge plates create a wide tail for swimming

2×2 brick with two ball joints

2×2 brick with socket

BENDY BODY

Pieces with ball and socket joints form the base of the sea serpent's long body. These connections let it bend and flex.

COOL CRATER SQUID

Make some space for an intergalactic pet made from your LEGO collection! No one knows whether life on other planets exists or what it might look like, so aim for the moon with your ideas.

Eye love my pet crater squid!

Printed eyes fit onto the tips of dinosaur tails

Four macaroni tiles form the crater's opening

You could build another small pet to live here

PINNED DOWN

A LEGO Technic block holds the alien's tentacles. It connects to a 2×2 tile with pin inside the crater.

1×3×3 LEGO Technic pin connector block

2×2 tile with pin

CUTE CLAWED CREATURE

Feeling crabby? Cheer yourself up with an adorable clawed companion like this space creature. With moving eye stalks, pincers, and posable legs, your LEGO pet is ready for playtime any time.

BUILD TIP!

Add the creature's bendy legs last. This will stop them falling off as you build.

Clips let the eye stalks move up and down

Curved slopes make crab-like claws

Knee joints bend on ball and socket plates

Plate with clip

I'm a building star!

CLIP AND GO
The alien's legs clip onto a 2×2 round plate with octagonal bar. They can be moved around the body.

HEROIC HIPPOGRIFF

Mix and match different parts of animals to create a famous mythical creature, such as this hippogriff (half eagle, half horse). Or come up with a mixed-up creature you've never heard of before!

Strong wings are made from long angled plates

A 1×2 plate with bar forms the horselike tail

BUILD TIP!

Build in sections, such as the head, legs, and torso. Connect them to create a creature.

1×1 plates with clips look like an eagle's talons

WING IT

Plates with bars beneath the angled plates connect the bird's wings to the clips in the model's body.

Clip

1×1 plate with bar

MAGICAL SHEEP

Who says you can't have a rainbow sheep for a pet? This miniature model is shaped like a sheep, but the colorful pieces that form its woolly coat add a touch of magic. What powers would the colors give your pet?

My pet has magical painting powers!

1×1 slope ear attaches to a brick with side stud in the head

Legs are made from 1×1 cones stacked on 1×1 round plates

1×1 brick with side stud

2×4 plate

INNER CORE

The sheep's tail and woolly coat attach to bricks with side studs in the sheep's middle.

1×2 jumper plate connects to a brick with side studs

DREAMY DRAGON

Fire up your building skills and make yourself a fantastic pet dragon! Remember to give your legendary lizard-like creature large wings so it can soar off on grand adventures.

Transparent pieces add a magical look

To the store for more dragon chow!

Feet are stacks of bricks and plates on their sides

Round tiles for the dragon's scaly skin

OPEN UP

The dragon's jaw is built on plates with clips and bars. These pieces let the mouth open and close.

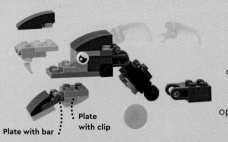

Plate with bar

Plate with clip

BUILD TIP!

If you want a flexible tail like this one, use click hinges so it can bend.

Tail spikes sit on top of click hinge plates

Movable wings are angled hinge plates

FLYING FELINE

Turn your LEGO household pets into superheroes! This incredible cat has two long wedge plate wings that can move up and down. What sorts of super powers will your pets have?

This is a truly super build!

Upside-down 1×1 heart tile makes a super adorable cat nose

3×6 wedge plates form superhero wings

1×1 plate with clip is a useful claw for grabbing objects

AMAZING WINGS

Ball and socket pieces form the base of the cat's wings. The wedge plates on top give them an aerodynamic look.

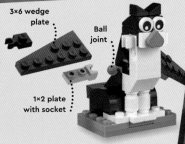

3×6 wedge plate

Ball joint

1×2 plate with socket

WELCOMING WEREWOLF

Perhaps you'd like to take care of a monstrous pet, such as a werewolf. He might look wild with his sharp fangs and large claws, but he's actually very friendly. Don't forget to build him a snazzy outfit, too.

1×1 rounded plates with bars look like ears

What else should I wear tonight?

Fangs are made from plates with teeth

LEGO Technic pin

Brick with hole

BUILD TIP!

Build clothes and accessories on top of the body so you can change them as needed.

HOLE CONNECTION

Bricks with holes are built into the tops of each leg. They fit onto LEGO Technic pins.

BONY BEAST

If you like things that are inside out, then a brick-built skeleton pet might be for you! Use spindly white pieces to create a bony creature of any kind. This beast looks like a bony-winged dragon.

BUILD TIP!

Stand models with long pieces like this one on plates to stop them from tipping over.

Poles make even the wings look like thin bones

A stack of 1×1 bricks forms a long spine

Clips and bars look like bony joints

HORNED HEAD

Barbs and cattle horns crown the head of this skeleton for an extra spiky look. Tooth pieces would work, too.

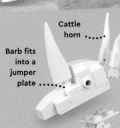

Cattle horn ......

Barb fits into a jumper plate ......

SOLID PET ROCK

Here's a pet that rocks! You could use gray pieces to form a rock with eyes and a mouth, or build an animal into a rocky wall like this. The animal can be changed by rearranging the plates.

Different slopes create a jagged stone wall

BUILT IN

A variety of plates form the horse in the wall. The plates that make the legs are stacked sideways.

2×4 plate

1×2 plate

Use small plates to design pictures of animals

This pet is very quiet . . .

ENCHANTING ELEPHANT

An elephant would be an amazing animal companion. One with wheels could be truly extraordinary! This brick-built pet has tires for speeding off on adventures and space for a minifigure, too.

Large ears are two 3×3 round corner plates

Base of the elephant's bendy trunk is a 1×3×2 arch

This brick-built pet is a winner!

1×1 quarter circle tiles give the face a rounded shape

Driver's seat can hold a minifigure or carry supplies

BUILD TIP!

Build plates with wheel connectors into the base so you can add tires.

2×2 curved slopes form smooth, solid sides

Four small tires roll along the ground

DELIGHTFUL DETAILS

Features such as tails make animal builds instantly recognizable. This tail is made from a robot arm.

1×2 jumper plate

Robot arm

Find the carrot on page 77.

CHAPTER 3
CREATURE COMFORTS

I'm bowled over by how much fun this is!

HOPPY HUTCH

Your brick-built buddies need a place to call home! Be sure to build cozy pet buildings, such as this rabbit hutch, where creatures can rest and relax. This one even has a rooftop garden!

Plant leaves offer snacks and shade for the pets

Who wants a snack?

Slopes make sturdy frames

Green plates form a comfortable, grassy base

FEET FIRST

Three 1×1 rounded plates with bars form the feet. They keep the bunny safely connected to the sunny rooftop garden.

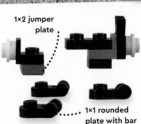

1×2 jumper plate

1×1 rounded plate with bar

LEAFY LOUNGE

Camouflaging chameleons like this one hang out where they can blend in with their surroundings. Build a home in colors that match your lizard so you can have fun playing hide-and-seek.

BUILD TIP!

Plant elements make great hideaways. Look for leaf pieces in any color.

Plant grass stem tail blends in with the lush background

Orange 1×1 round plate with leaves matches one of the lizard's bright colors

Plates make a sturdy base for the leafy home

HOLD ON

Four skeleton arm pieces form the legs. The clips connect the lizard's feet to a bar.

Skeleton arm

Bar with stopper

COZY CHICKEN COOP

Here's an egg-cellent place for hens to live! Henhouses like this one need four walls and a roof to keep pet hens warm and safe. Don't forget to add a ramp so the birds can easily enter and exit the building.

One 6×8 slope forms a large part of the roof

Tiles fit onto bricks with side studs to make walls

Ramp is a 2×3 tile with clips, which can fold up and down

Latticed window lets sunlight and fresh air inside

PERFECT PERCH

The hens' eggs can rest safely in an egg box made from a brown plate at the center of the coop.

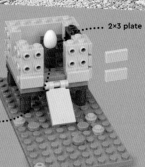

2×3 plate

1×1 round brick

PLEASANT PIGPEN

Happy hogs love a muddy pen like this one. Use bars of any size to make the fence panels as big or as small as you want. And be sure to add plenty of brown plates to the ground so the pigs have mud to play in.

BUILD TIP!

Build the base first so you can see how wide or narrow the pen needs to be.

I never get boar-ed of building!

2×3 tile with clips is a gate that opens and closes

Green plates look like farmyard grasses

1×1 round plates with holes support the fence posts

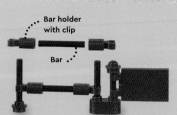

Bar holder with clip

Bar

ON THE FENCE

Bars form the fence's rails. Bar holders with clips connect each section of rails to the next one.

FIN-TASTIC FISH TANK

Make a splash with an impressive brick-built tank for your fish. Attach your fish models to stacks of transparent bricks to make it look as though they are gliding through the water. Remember to add plants and rocks, too!

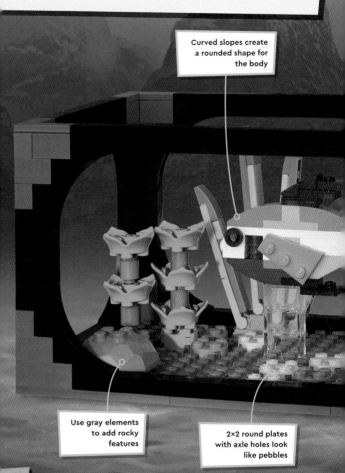

Curved slopes create a rounded shape for the body

Use gray elements to add rocky features

2×2 round plates with axle holes look like pebbles

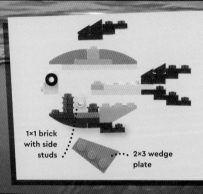

FINNED FRIEND

Just one wedge plate creates a pectoral fin for this goldfish. It fits onto a 1×1 brick with side studs in the fish's body.

1×1 brick with side studs

2×3 wedge plate

BUILD TIP!

Attach decorative pieces, such as plants, to the base of your tank before you build the walls.

Dive in for building fun!

BUG BANDSTAND

Do your LEGO® pets have any hobbies? These minibeast models love to belt out a tune. There is plenty of space on the stage for their buggy band to play. What would you build for your pet?

Radar dishes turn the flower into a speaker

Plates built into the stem form platforms

BUILD TIP!

Make sure tall stacks of bricks are built on baseplates to stop them from tumbling down.

Stack of 2×2 bricks forms the stage's stem

MUSIC MACHINE
Small pieces, including printed round tiles, create a disco deck for the fly to spin records on as the band plays.

1×1 round plate with bar

Printed round tile records

LUNAR LEAP PAD

Whether your pet is from Earth or elsewhere in the universe, they'll need a place to exercise and play! This moonlike surface has crater-shaped rings for a pet space critter to jump across. How quickly can she do the course?

Flag marker for navigating the course

Can I have a try?

Stack plates to form different levels

1×1 round tiles look like little moon rocks

2×2 macaroni tile

2×2 round tile with hole

CRATER CREATOR

Each crater in the scene is made from rounded tiles attached to plates.

PEACEFUL CAMPSITE

Build a relaxing campground for your pets. You don't even have to leave home! Make sure there are plenty of comfy places to sleep, such as tents and hammocks. And don't forget to bring your pets some treats!

Stack of 1×1 round bricks forms the tree's trunk

I hope that marshmallow is for me!

HANG ON

Four skeleton arms form the hammock's "ropes." Clips connect the hammock to the support poles.

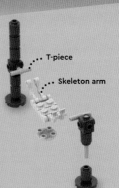

T-piece

Skeleton arm

6×6 tiles are held at angles by hinge bricks and plates at the base

BUILD TIP!

Add tall models, such as trees, to the scene last. This will stop them toppling as you build.

Who's sleeping in the pup tent?

Use brown bricks and pieces to build a bright, glowing campfire

BUMPY HORSE TRAIL

Horses—even LEGO ones—need lots of exercise every day. Let them trot along a mountainous trail. This one is made from plates, which means you can easily extend or shorten the path.

BUILD TIP!

LEGO horses are two studs wide. Make sure your pets can fit on the trail.

Don't horse around—get building!

Add flowers and plant pieces

Narrow plates at the edges of the path hold the baseplates together

2×2 brick

1×4 curved slope

BRICK-BUILT BUSHES

Stacks of bricks, plates, and curved slopes on the far side of the trail form leafy hedges.

COMFY COUCH

All pets deserve a comfortable place to curl up for a nap or to sit and rest. Design a couch, chair, or bed that suits your pet's needs. A pampered pooch might enjoy scrumptious snacks on a sofa like this one.

I'm glad the couch isn't so far away!

Two 1×3 curved slopes shape the back of the couch

Four legs are 1×1 round plates

Couch cushions are made from 2×2 tiles

PLATE UP

The base of the couch is made of two layers of narrow plates. They stack onto the four legs.

1×2 plate

1×8 plate

SUPER SLIDE

Would your LEGO pet feel at home at a water park? This water snake sure does! There are steps and slides to slither along as well as a big pool to swim in. Get building and make a splash!

BUILD TIP!

Check the height of the slides before building the stairs. This way you can build stairs to the right level.

Connect bricks along one row of studs to make stairs

6×6×6 playground slide makes a good water slide

Water we going to build today?

1×1 transparent round plates for splashy water

AWESOME ARCHWAYS

Three 1×6×2 arches form tunnel entrances to a hideaway in the middle of the pool.

1×6×2 arch ......

16×16 plate ......

FABULOUS FISH PALACE

Make your pet sea creatures feel like royalty with a palatial home, such as this castle. There are lots of tall windows for the fish to swim through, as well as a lovely underwater garden.

My fish are superstars!

Clips hold LEGO fish to make it look like they are swimming

Seaweed piece is held in place by a 1×1 round plate

6×6 radar dish

4×8 half circle plate forms part of the base

2×2 dome

STACK OF DISHES

Domes top three different sizes of radar dishes to form the roofs.

CHEERFUL PLAYROOM

Why not create a whole room dedicated to fun for your LEGO pets? Build a room with two walls and fill it with all the brick-built toys and games you think your pets will like. What do your pets want to play with?

Bricks with side studs in the wall hold the toy shelf

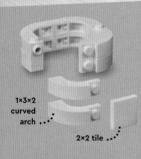

1×3×2 curved arch

2×2 tile

HAVE A BALL

Curved arches form the sides of the ball pit. Two tiles hold the rounded edges together.

Tiles cover plates to form a playful tent

Build just two walls for a room like this one. It will give you more space to play with your pets.

Tiles top stacks of bricks in the walls for a finished look

2×4 tiles are mattresses in this pet bunk bed

Some bunny looks very sleepy!

Cute crab rests on a 1×1 plate on the chair's arm

1×1 round plates make "balls" for this ball pit

FANCIFUL FOREST

Instead of a traditional forest, build your LEGO companions a colorful woodland. Jewels and sparkly and transparent pieces add a touch of magic to the scene.

BUILD TIP!

Look for colorful plant pieces, such as pink leaves, to create a magical woodland.

Curly gray plant stems create fairy-tale features

Purple plates add color to the forest floor

Use jewel pieces to invent magical plants

BRANCH OUT

The sturdy branches on the bejeweled trees are different sized arches. They connect to a trunk made from round bricks.

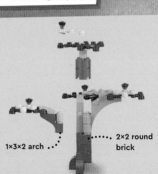

1×3×2 arch ····

···· 2×2 round brick

PERFECT PET ROOMS

Build a whole house for your pets—one room at a time! Each small space can stand alone or be joined together to form a large home. Just make sure the builds are the right size so your pets can fit inside.

Printed round tile is a toilet seat for potty trained pets

Remove tiles to stack a room on top of this one

Stack up bricks as high as you like to make walls

I'm not so sure about the artwork...

2×2 curved slope

4×6 plate

COVER UP

Four 2×2 curved slopes form a patterned quilt on this lucky dog's bed. Curved slopes also make the pillows.

ADORABLE ABODE

Why not build a home for your pet that looks just like them? A snail would love living in this house, which is built to look just like the mini mollusk. Remember to add creature comforts, such as windows.

BUILD TIP!

Think about the animal's features and how they can be used as part of a house.

1×1 cones hold bars to create the snail's eye stalks

Large radar dish makes a shell-like roof

There's even a mailbox for snail mail!

FOUNDATION AFOOT

Two rounded plates create a sturdy base. They also form the shape of a snail's foot.

8×8 rounded plate

TASTY TREATS

Don't forget to feed your creatures healthy meals and tempting treats. What do your LEGO pets like to munch on? They might like fresh fruits and veggies, a bowl of food, or something else!

Never put LEGO pieces in your mouth!

A unicorn might like a cookie with a magical jam center

Carrot top is made from 3×4 plant leaves

Four 3×3 round corner bricks form the bowl's sides

2×2 round brick

LEGO Technic axle with grooves

2×2 dome

IN THE GROOVE

One LEGO Technic axle with grooves connects the stack of round bricks that form the carrot to the dome at the top.

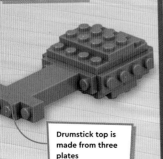

Drumstick top is made from three plates

BRICK TYPES

When you're planning your pet models it can be helpful to know which LEGO® pieces you have and what they are called. These are just some of the many LEGO parts you may come across. If you don't have all of these pieces, don't worry! You can make lots of models with the elements you do have.

What brick will I pick?

⚠ Small parts and small balls can cause choking if swallowed. Not for children under 3 years.

MEASUREMENTS

The size of a LEGO piece is described by the number of studs it has. A brick that has two studs across and three studs up is called a 2×3 brick. Tall parts have a third number, which is the height of the piece in standard bricks.

2×3 brick
top view

2×3 brick
side view

1×1×3 brick
side view

BRICKS

Bricks are the basis of most builds. They come in many shapes, sizes, and colors.

2×2 brick

2×2 round brick

1×2 brick

PLATES

Plates have studs on top and tubes on the bottom, but plates are thinner than bricks. Three stacked plates are the same height as one standard brick.

3 stacked 1×2 plates next to a 1×2 brick

2×3 plate

1×1 plate

JUMPER PLATES

These plates have just one stud in the middle, and they let you "jump" the usual grid of LEGO studs. These pieces are useful for centering things in your models.

2×2 jumper plate   1×2 jumper plate

TILES

Tiles have tubes on the bottom and no studs on top. These parts give your builds a smooth finish, and printed tiles add more detail.

2×2 tile   Printed eye tile

SIDE STUDS

Pieces with studs on more than one side let you build outward as well as upward.

1×1 brick with side stud   1×2/2×2 bracket

CLIPS

Pieces with clips can attach to other elements, such as bars.

1×1 plate with clip   1×2 plate with bar

JOINTS

Add flexibility to your build with parts that have balls and sockets.

1×2 plate with socket   1×2 plate with ball joint

LEGO® TECHNIC

These elements expand the range of functions you can build into your models. They are particularly useful for builds with lots of moving parts or technical details.

LEGO® Technic pin   LEGO Technic axle

SLOPES

Slope bricks have diagonal angles. They can be curved or inverted (upside down).

1×1 slope   1×2 inverted slope

1×3 curved slope

HINGES

Add movement to your builds with hinge pieces. Hinge plates and hinge bricks let parts of your builds move from side to side or tilt up and down.

1×2 hinge brick with 2×2 hinge plate (side view)   1×2 click hinge plates

DK | Penguin Random House

Senior Editor Tori Kosara
Project Art Editor Jenny Edwards
Production Editor Marc Staples
Senior Production Controller Lloyd Robertson
Managing Editor Paula Regan
Managing Art Editor Jo Connor
Publishing Director Mark Searle

Inspirational models built by
Mariann Asanuma, Jason Briscoe, Emily Corl, Nate Dias, Jessica Farrell,
Rod Gillies, Tim Goddard, Kevin Hall, Barney Main, and Simon Pickard

Photography by Gary Ombler
Designed for DK by Thelma-Jane Robb
Cover design by James McKeag

Dorling Kindersley would like to thank:
Randi Sørensen, Heidi K. Jensen, Lydia Barram, Paul Hansford,
Martin Leighton Lindhart, and Nina Koopmann at the LEGO Group.
DK also thanks Julia March for proofreading; Selina Wood for
editorial assistance; and Megan Douglass for Americanizing.

First American Edition, 2024
Published in the United States by DK Publishing
1745 Broadway, 20th Floor, New York, NY 10019

Page design copyright © 2024 Dorling Kindersley Limited
DK, a Division of Penguin Random House LLC
24 25 26 27 28 10 9 8 7 6 5 4 3 2 1
001–338683–Feb/2024

A catalog record for this book
is available from the Library of Congress

ISBN 978-0-7440-9220-2

Printed and bound in China

www.dk.com
www.LEGO.com

MIX
Paper | Supporting
responsible forestry
FSC™ C018179
www.fsc.org

This book was made with Forest
Stewardship Council™ certified
paper – one small step in DK's
commitment to a sustainable future.
For more information go to
www.dk.com/our-green-pledge